Some Women's Lives

Tamar Diana Wilson

Plain View Press
P. O. 42255
Austin, TX 78704

plainviewpress.net
sb@plainviewpress.net
512-441-2452

Copyright Tamar Diana Wilson 2010. All rights reserved.
ISBN: 978-1-935514-48-0
Library of Congress Number: 2010922428

Cover art by Michael Hoffee
Cover design by Susan Bright

Acknowledgments

The following poems included herein were previously published.

1993. "Tijuana, 1965" in. *Saturday Afternoon Journal* No.9, pp. 103-104.

1993. "From L.A. to New York, Cadiz, Marseilles, Frankfurt, London. . . ." in *Struggle: A Magazine of Proletarian Revolutionary Literature*. Vol. 9, No. 3, pp. 2-4.

1997 (Autumn) "Newcomer" Thema/ "Too Proud to Ask" Vol. 9 No.3, pp. 47-48. Metairie, Louisiana: THEMA Literary Society.

I would like to thank the editors of those journals for publishing my work as well as Susan Bright of *Plain View Press* with overseeing onward several of my books.

.

for women everywhere

Contents: Some Women's Lives

Mexico

Mujer Ingrata (Ungrateful Woman)	9
"Venga Alma. Haga éste cuarto"	10
Pesos*	12
Mexicana Beach Vendors	14
Grey-Green Onyx Figurines	15
Serapes	16
The Washerwoman	19
Celestina and Her Daughters	21
The Widow Angela	28
Borderlines	30
Cast Iron Fence	32
"My Only Regret . . ."	34
Tijuana, 1965	36

Los Angeles

From L.A. to New York, Cadiz, Marseilles, Frankfurt, London . . .	41
Sawtelle Boulevard, West L.A.	45
Garments	49
Rosario	50
Newcomer	53
My Neighbor, Noreen	55

Port City Women

Butterflies	59
Seamen's Girls	62
Migrant Women	64
Three Dollars	66
A Dollar a Drink	68
Decatur Street	70

Elsewhere's Women

"La Vibora"   75
Catch   76
Turquoise and Silver, 1999   78
The Witch   79
Faded Purple   80
Clash   82

Fragments Of an Autobiography

Reading Allen Ginsberg's Reading Bai Juyi-I   85
Fleeting Honeymoon   87
Drugs   88
Monadic Me   89
Love At First Glance   90
Upon Reading Pope's Reading Of Horace's Ode I   91
So You Want Me Back?   93
En Fin   94
After He Moved On   96
Cross-Border Love Canals   97
Like Widowhood   99
Alone On the Shore   100
You Were My River   102
Past Pleasures   103
Upon Reaching Sixty   105
Elsewhere's Other Autumns   106

About the Author   111

Mexico

Mujer Ingrata (Ungrateful Woman)

San Miguel de Allende, Guanajuato 2003

A woman, begging, murmured *"mujer ingrata"*
when I passed the doorway where she rests
on Canal Street near La Iglesia de las Monjas
because I had no coins in my pocket
nor patience to rummage in my purse.

I should be more generous, she must have meant
with my new navy slacks and cardigan
with my leather shoes and *mochila* filled with stuff
she does not own: books, notebooks, camera, pens
and two thousand dollars in traveler's checks.

I should have more gratitude
for possessing such great resources. I should
pass some on, to the aged hovering in doorways
who eat only tortillas and *frijoles* day after day
and live in hovels with no electric lights.

I turn some bills into change
at the Tecolote Bookstore near San Miguel's
and to the next two women, grey-haired,
aproned, hands outstretched
I give each ten pesos

not enough.

"Venga Alma. Haga éste cuarto"

>San Miguel de Allende, Guanajuato 2003

She'll be sixty years old in June, Doña Alma:
She works cleaning rooms in *la posada*
up the street from the church of *las monjas*.
She's worked there twenty-five years,
now earns four dollars a day,
a bit above Guanajuato's minimum wage.
She worries her pension will be very low:
She hopes to retire some months from now.

She's proud of her son and four daughters:
Not one of them went wrong,
though one daughter married a man, Alma's *yerno*
who shouts at her and their children
after drinking bouts that last for days.
"She should leave him," says Doña Alma.

One daughter is a nurse, another a Spanish teacher,
a third owns a restaurant along with her husband;
her son runs a grocery with the help of his wife.
Hard workers all like their mother Alma
who garners twenty-four dollars a week plus tips
and hosts her eight grandchildren Sunday afternoons,
seventeen the eldest, a *señorita*, two years the youngest, a *varón*.

All this Doña Alma tells me
while she sweeps the carpet, fetches water,
makes the beds, cleans the bathroom sink and floor.
I sit and listen and add my questions
and wonder why some can pay more for one night's lodging
than Alma earns for a week's worth of working.

And as we talk she hurries
broom or mop or dustcloth in hand,

her greying hair bound back, patience in her eyes,
with much cleaning to do in the *posada*,
and throughout the afternoon the *mayordomo* cries,
"*Venga Alma. Haga éste cuarto.*"

A modest breakfast at Correo's with coffee
costs more than she earns a day
like Doña Julia who hand makes tortillas
at a Puerto Vallarta café,
but couldn't afford the cheapest dinner
with only one day's wage.

Doña Alma moves rapidly, from one room to another,
she has no time to rest.
If she pauses just one moment, someone shouts,
"*Venga Alma. Haga éste cuarto…*"

A Huichol couple, Puerto Vallarta, 2003.

Pesos*

                              Puerta Vallarta, Jalisco 2002

Puerta Vallarta, *Zona Romántica*:
The street of cafés they call Basilio Badillo
then along the beach, restaurant *tras* restaurant
Daquiri Dick's and Hotel Playa los Arcos.

At one sidewalk café
all you can eat is offered
for only *setenta* pesos:
Ribs, beef, chicken, chorizo and more.

At Roberto's Mariscos
two stories high, haunt of expatriates,
all variety of seafood starts
at 99 pesos goes up to 345.

Across the street
pollo en molé is fifty pesos
and *chimichangas* fifty-five
the best deal on the street of cafés.

On their outdoor terrace,
Doña Julia hand makes corn tortillas
six days a week over a hot grill:
She makes forty pesos a shift.

And the hotel maids can only
inhale *sabores* from the stoves:
For six days work their salary is 370 pesos,
less than dinner and drinks for two at Roberto's.

You can swim with the dolphins for one thousand three hundred
or ride horseback to a waterfall for half of that
and the guides count themselves lucky:
they earn two hundred pesos a day.

* * * * *

As I eat all you can for *setenta* pesos
small boys and girls pass among the tables
sell chicklets at a dollar a package
or a single red rose for the same.

A boy child of six or seven
passes by my table where there's all you can eat
selling bobbing head and tailed *tortugas*
accepts a tortilla and a small rack of ribs,

calls over the flower girl who has scurried
along the beach and up and down five or six streets.
She extends her hand, if she can't sell me roses:
she smiles as I give her some leftovers.

---

* *Peso* has two meanings in Mexico: it is the name of the money used, but it also means "weight" or "burden" with implications of "sorrow." At the time of writing the peso exchange was 10 to a dollar.

Mexicana Beach Vendors

Los Cabos, 2008

They carry ceramics, beaded necklaces and knick knacks,
they display dresses and skirts made of Indonesian cloth,
they resell silver bracelets and t-shirts and blankets.

They come from Oaxaca, they come from Guerrero,
they come from distant *ranchos* and *pueblos*,
they come to the coasts to sell things by the sea.

Women with children and women of age:
They vend their wares along the beachfronts
populated by tourists upon whom they gaze.

Patricia walks on the beach in Cabo San Lucas
sells the sundresses she has sewn
from lengths of cloth bought from an importer.

Alicia is strong from lugging plates and bowls
—many of which she and her family have painted—
up and down the long strand in *Pueblo Viejo*.

Leticia scouts the tourists in Rosarito
her three children following in her wake:
She sells bracelets throughout that beach town.

Some have husbands who do the same work,
some have children who sell knick knacks and gum,
some are widowed or abandoned or alone.

They vend their ceramics, beadwork and knick knacks,
they display the dresses and silver bracelets,
they walk in the hot sand along lengthy beaches.

Grey-Green Onyx Figurines

>   Los Cabos, 2002

Anita comes to kneel by our table, wears an orange apron dress,
in one of the myriad restaurant-bars that line the boulevard.
And from plastic bags she takes out small onyx dolphins,
lines them up in diminishing size, then turtles,
elephants, frogs all lined up in their six different sizes,
asks us to buy the grey-green hand-carved figurines.

Anita came here eleven years ago, her sister brought them she said,
brought her and her two younger sisters and brother,
after her father was killed in a Guerrero rebellion,
out in the countryside, after he was shot down. And they wander
together, the four of them, selling their onyx figurines along
the boulevard and on the marina and on the beach.

Anita married when she was seventeen, she said,
and has a son and is pregnant again, though she looks
fifteen or even younger, my friend Patty says. And her
husband is from Guerrero too, sells ceramic plates at
San José hotels while Anita and her siblings sell
tiny onyx statues in restaurants and bars and on the marina,

those bar-restaurants that line the main street of Los Cabos,
home to expatriates, tourists, and vendors of trinkets.
"All of us on the beach are from Guerrero," says Anita,
"In Acapulco there is no more work." Then she puts her
stone figures back in their bags, and she and her sisters
and baby brother skip across and down the street.

She'll walk all day and she'll seldom sit,
she'll kneel by your table and show you her dolphins,
elephants, turtles, and frogs, naming them in an Indian idiom.
Smiling at the English word, she looks like a child and she
carries a child under the apron that covers her slight body
as she skips away down the street to the next *cantina*.

Serapes

                    Oaxaca, 1988

Isabel and her mother both make fine serapes,
weave the black cloth striped in red and gold.
Isabel and her mother both live on a *rancho*
three hours walking and two hours by bus
from Oaxaca, the capital city.

Isabel and her mother carry on their heads
fifteen serapes each one:
Walk down the mountain, walk through the forest,
catch the only bus that passes each day
to their destination, Oaxaca City.

They sell their serapes for one hundred pesos,
they sell their serapes to earn a small income,
they sell their serapes to tourists,
Mexican, American, European,
who lunch, drink, or dine in the plaza.

At night they sleep on a quiet street
surrounded by serapes unsold.
Once they are gone Isabel and her mother
return to their *rancho* once more
two hours by bus, three hours walking.

There is no electricity where they live,
no schools past second grade.
Husbands and fathers work on their *milpas*,
grow corn for tortillas and also sow beans,
while the women weave black, red and gold serapes.

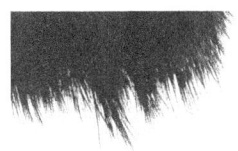

Woman selling beadwork, Puerto Vallarta, 2004.

Woman selling Indonesian clothe with Mexican designs, Puerto Vallarta, 2004.

Beach vendor selling ceramics, Puerto Vallarta, 2004.

Vendors on the marina, Cabo San Lucas, 2008.

Woman vendor on the marina, Cabo San Lucas, 2008.

The Washerwoman

> "Los Arboles," Jalisco 1990

Antonia goes from house to house
asks if there are clothes to wash.
She'll take them home, launder them in a tub,
hang them on her long clothes line,
iron them, fold them, carry them back again.

Or she'll go to the homes of the *ejidatarios*
or to those who own some land
clean their sheets in their washing machines
with the help of her retarded daughter:
that's how they stay alive.

A decade or slightly more ago
her husband crossed to California
left the *rancho*, his wife and child,
to seek a job somewhere:
worked in the vineyards of Mendocino and Ukiah.

He'd go to the bars on Saturday night
and after some years in *los Estados Unidos*
he took up with another woman.
He stopped sending money orders home,
that's how Antonia became a washerwoman.

Three years ago he returned:
Antonia did not want to see him.
He lured her to her Aunt Cuca's house
claimed her as his wife
then promptly left again.

continued…

Now Antonia has a two-year-old son
besides her daughter seventeen.
She roams around the *rancho*
looks for dirty laundry:
She's never heard from him again.

Harvest times she begs for a job
cuts corn from stalks now yellowed.
She raises chickens and some turkeys
she sells their eggs and works in the beanfields,
but she's known as the *rancho*'s washerwoman.

Celestina and Her Daughters

                    "Los Arboles," Jalisco 1990

Celestina and her husband have seven daughters:
They lament that they had no son.
Celestina's husband is a sharecropper:
He also drinks from sunrise on,
so the work falls to her and her girls.

Celestina and her family live in an adobe house
In two rooms of four, the other two crumbling.
They store their corn in the back patio
to feed their chickens, to make tortillas,
to sell in exchange for potatoes and beans.

Celestina's husband sharecrops four *hectareas*
of cornfields for an absentee owner.
Celestina and their daughters are his workforce:
They plant, hoe, harvest and carry the crop
Under the Jalisco sun.

Celestina's husband is angry
because he cannot provide.
So he sulks and he drinks
and sometimes he beats her
or yells and storms his hurt pride.

Though Celestina and her daughters
do the work called that of men
plant, hoe, harvest and carry the crop,
a husband, father, or son is needed
to gain access to sharecropping land.

                                          continued…

Celestina and her daughters go to the fields,
Celestina's husband feels ashamed.
Lack of land, lack of sons, what a misfortune,
his women working in public places
tending crops in his name.

That's why he occasionally beats her:
To remind her who is *jefe:*.
Otherwise he's a man without honor
on a *rancho* where most men of means
keep their wives and daughters confined.

Migrant workers from Zacatecas in "Los Arboles," Jalisco, 1990.

A woman migrant worker at the "Los Arboles" corn harvest, 1990.

Sharecropper's wife and daughters harvesting corn in "Los Arboles," 1990.

Sharcropper's wife shelling corn, "Los Arboles," 1990.

A sharecropper family's share of corn, "Los Arboles," 1990.

An ejidatario's daughter in her father's cornfields, "Los Arboles," 1990.

Woman pressing corn tortillas, Puerto Vallarta, 2005.

Woman toasting corn tortillas, Puerto Vallarta, 2003.

Separating beans, "Los Arboles," 1990.

Ejidatario's wife separating beans, "Los Arboles," 1990.

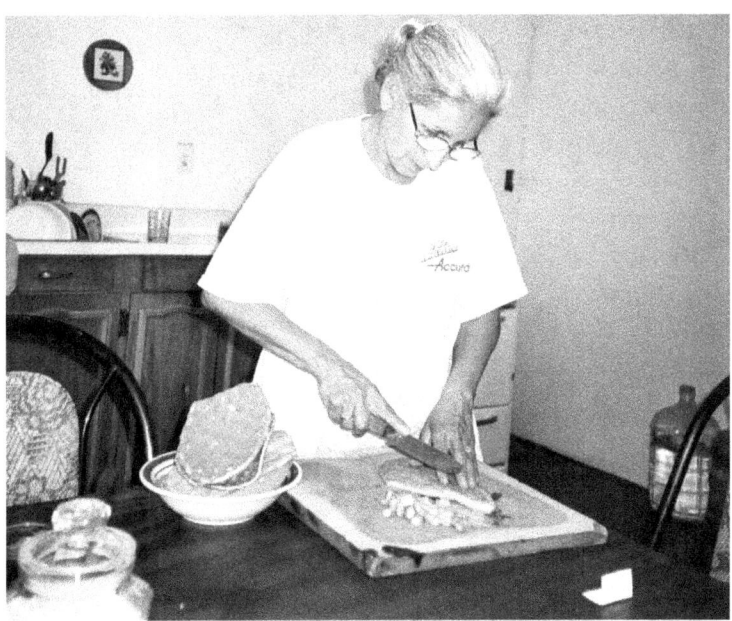
Preparing nopales, "Colonia Popular," Mexicali, 2003.

The Widow Angela

> "Los Arboles," Jalisco 1990

Doña Angela pauses from hoeing her vegetable garden
her eighteen grandchildren like doves flitting around her
comes to the front of her dark adobe home
built by the family on their own plot of ground:
We sit beside her outdoor oven while she toasts tortillas
made with corn milled from last year's harvest.

"We left our birthplace in Zacatecas,
tumbled like cotton bolls north to Durango, then again south
until we found lands to sharecrop here on this Jalisco *rancho*:
each child was a helping hand.
But sharecropping dried up when tractors and threshers came in
then Juan died and we were left like field mice without grain.

"So first my eldest, then my next
flew like wild flocks toward the polar star
fled like the geese to their northern abodes
dispersed to that other land
picked golden and ruby apples, they say
with my brother's sons in Michigan.

"Then they drifted to Milwaukee, that's in Wisconsin,
where Juan's uncle Rodolfo lived
flitted like moths to the fires
of an automobile parts foundry
filled molds with molten steel—
at least that's what they told me.

"Later they called my youngest ones
with seductive stories of higher wages there
than near here in Guadalajara. Their sweat no longer
fertilizes the corn but drips into metals cooling.
And I, I sit with my daughters-in-law
while we share an emptiness like dying.

"But they do return like the flying geese
when winter is wearing it's last lust
and bring us sweaters, cassettes, videos
and liven our lives with their stories.
Then the cross once more in the long bitter spring
while their children grow like *guajes*.

"It is as though they had been ripped from my womb
and smashed against some foreign shale.
It is as though they had been torn from my breast
and drowned in the Río Bravo.
That's the way it is until they return
like the wild flocks to their winter's nest."

Borderlines

                    Mexicali. Baja California 1991

Bright intermittent colors like fields of multi-specied flowers,
turquoise, red, orange, yellow, striped, royal blue:
Pieces, patches of discarded garments, many unstained and whole,
appear among trash and food scraps, broken furniture, bent utensils,
rusting metals, and whatever other garbage has been disposed
in Mexicali's garbage dump, where Ramona is gleaning
with the help of her eight year old Ramón and six year old Amalia.

Ramona reaches toward a tied plastic bag, rips it, tears it, opens it
with a bent nail set in a long wooden handle:
Looks for aluminum beer and soda cans or electric wiring
from which to strip the copper—metals for resale, recyclying,
so she can buy beans, tortillas, salt, maybe even chilis,
and with luck two notebooks and pens
so her children can go back to school again.

She moves to a pile of clothing, men's, women's and children's,
chooses a few skirts and blouses for herself and her sister Dora,
a red sweater for her son Ramón, then carefully inspects
scattered pants, shirts and dresses:
Selects them, folds them, stuffs them
into her large cloth bag made of scraps.
She'll wash them, she'll iron them,
she'll give them as gifts, she'll use them as cleaning rags,
she'll hawk them from door to door.

A mattress, not too dirty, Ramona drags to one side:
She's just found another bed, so the children can sleep alone.
A cardboard box filled with vegetables from the supermarket:
She pulls off the wilted leaves and has a small head of cabbage;
the tomatoes have only small rotten spots,
she'll take them home too,
along with a bonus for the day: discarded fish heads from the
fish vendor with which she will make a stew.

Her daughter Amalia then calls: "Look here mamá" and points
to a box filled with shoes. Ramona looks and admires them:
Though she has nowhere to wear purple suede high heels
nor golden sandals with a wedge, she'll take them along just in case
someone might want to buy them. And luckily enough there is
a pair of high-topped sneakers, black and only slightly worn,
that in the next year or so will fit her growing son Ramón.

The next find of the day is a tortilla press,
slightly loose at the handle;
it will help Ramona to save a bit of money:
Instead of buying ready made tortillas, packaged in the local store,
she can buy the much cheaper *nixtamal*,
although it will cost her several hours of chore.
And then: a large blue bunny rabbit, not too smudged or soiled,
To give to her Amalia.

Woman working in the Mexicali dump I 1991.

Cast Iron Fence

> Mexicali, Baja California 1991

Rosí was only fifteen and three months pregnant
when she first climbed the fourteen foot fence
that separated Mexicali from Calexico:
Her husband awaited her in the parking lot
beside the Peso Market.

José had gotten his provisional papers
just some years before
when his father, born in Brawley
returned after eleven years
from his work in Salinas.

A year passed before Rosí returned
to visit her mother and father
now with a four month old baby boy:
An American citizen
she proudly presented them.

Rosí plans to come every six months:
Her husband crosses back with the baby
one with a green card, one with a birthright
Rosí will climb the cast iron fence
to join them.

Woman working in the Mexicali dump II, 1991.

Doña Eulalia's store, rancho Los Arboles, 1989.

"My Only Regret . . ."

> Mexicali, Baja California 1993

"A friend of mine and I climbed the fence in Mexicali.
Then we walked to Indio."
Juanita said this simply, telling me of
her one and only trip to the U.S.A.

"What do you mean you walked to Indio?" I asked.
"That's two hours or more by car from Calexico.
Why didn't you go by Greyhound?"
The *migra* checks the buses though, we both knew.

"We had three dollars between us. Not enough to afford to eat.
But we picked some broccoli and some cabbage
between here and Westmoreland.
And some oranges near Calipatria."

"And for water?" I inquired, astounded.
"There's lots of irrigation canals along the way.
And sometimes we'd stop at houses. Only one woman
who spoke only English, ever sent us away."

"Whatever possessed you to walk to Indio?
Freezing nights in winter. Shimmering heat in summer?"
I insisted, still unbelieving, that this little woman
could have trudged more than one hundred miles.

"Well my husband left me, with a baby daughter.
My mother's been widowed a very long time.
My sisters are all married and not doing too well.
I have no brothers. I thought I'd look for a job."

"So you walked to Indio and found a job?" asked I, still amazed.
"We worked 12 hours a day in a warehouse, sweeping and cleaning,
piling up boxes of stuff. We had no place to live so at night
we'd stay behind some rolls of paper in the very same place."

"It was all right. It was o.k. We earned each day
what I earned a week in the electronics factory,
the one down by *La Ley*. But I missed my mother
and my baby daughter and my sisters too."

"But I guess the real reason I came back so soon,
was because the boss's brother
kept hanging around nights and not letting us sleep
and my friend said he even grabbed her while she was sweeping."

"And then there was an old man with nowhere to stay,
who said he'd just come from Los Angeles
where more people are living on the street every day.
Even more than in Mexico City.

"So a few months later, we came back, this time aboard a bus,
and I found this job in the assembly plant.
I'm glad I saw *el otro lado*
but my family's here so here I'll stay.

"We had a nice time all in all.
There was a toilet in the warehouse.
I still don't have one where I live now.
And there are things to tell my daughter about:

"That I was a tourist in *los Estados Unidos:*
I walked through their fields and ate from their orchards
I saw their long highways and hamburger stands
I lived in a vast warehouse and washed their new cars.

"Now I'm back to my *tierra* with its dirt roads
my dusty *colonia*, my family and friends.
And I'm quite well, thank you, here where I am.
My only regret is that I didn't see Disneyland."

Tijuana, 1965

                    Tijuana, Baja California

It was at the beginning of the Vietnam War
in a bar called Brooklyn in Tijuana
where the marines and sailors stationed in San Diego
came to drink and pick up bargirls
that I got to know Soccorro.

She had come from a *pueblo* in Zacatecas
where there was no work for women, little for men:
Her husband had hoped to cross into California
five years before
and she hadn't heard from him since then.
So she brought their two sons to that border city,
one six, one seven,

hoped someday to cross the frontier
perhaps to search for her husband
though she didn't know if he was still alive
or where he might be working;
But she had to continue, they had to eat,
so she went to a bar to earn a dollar a drink.

She drank with men, really boys, eighteen or so,
who came from small towns in Indiana or Idaho,
had never before seen another country
or even another state:
They were on their way to Vietnam
to see too much, too fast, too soon.

She went with a few, but very seldom,
and never to the next door hotel:
She took them to her two rented rooms
cooked them beans and made their meals
and stayed with them until troop carriers
carried them overseas.

She was pregnant when I met her
sitting on her barstool drinking cold tea
that looked like Scotch or Brandy:
She spoke of her life in Zacatecas;
Of men crossing the border to look for jobs;
And about the newest baby's father she told me:

"He was nineteen and from a small town,
probably like my own,
where everyone knew each other
and most everyone are cousins.
He joined the service and came to San Diego
and on his days off he'd come here."

"He bought me drinks and talked for some days.
He didn't have a girlfriend he said,
so he'd stay with me whenever he was on leave.
Then four months ago,
before we knew I was to bear his child,

he went to where they're fighting,
in that place called Vietnam.
He wrote to me in English
and I'd write to him in Spanish:
He answered my first letter,
but I haven't heard from him again.

She paused awhile and then she said:
"I don't know if he got my letter,
telling him I'm *esperando*,
that in early spring I'll have his child.
In any case he hasn't answered for at least two months or more."

continued…

She smiled, remembering Johnnie:
"He had blue eyes and blonde hair, you know.
He's probably found another woman.
At least I hope that's so.
It must be lonely over there
and he was very handsome."

This story is true, I swear to you,
It happened in November of '65.
More than five decades later
I wonder now and then
if Soccorro's still living in Tijuana
and if Johnnie ever saw his child.

Los Angeles

From L.A. to New York, Cadiz, Marseilles, Frankfurt, London . . .

Los Angeles, California 1988

you see them
        on buses
heads bobbing
        with fatigue
as they ride
        one hour or more   each way

to jobs
        in garment shops
        in electronics factories
        in metal foundries
        in old peoples' homes
        in construction cleanup
        load trucks
        mop hospital rooms
        make hotel beds
        as domestic servants
        as busboys
        as barmaids
        as dishwashers
        as fast food cooks and waitresses
        as fishermen and janitors
        as gardeners and caterers

sometimes they work a twelve hour day

then they return
        on buses
heads bobbing
        with fatigue
as they ride
        one hour or more   each way

continued…

to the ghettos where they live
        in apartments
        with leaky pipes
        radiators not working in winter
        plumbing not worth the metal
        electrical wiring frayed
        cracked windows
        creaking floors
        cockroaches
        rats

from jobs
        people
              say
        they are robbing
        from citizens
              say
        they don't pay enough taxes
        for all the services they use
              say
        they come in   invade
        cross borders   criminally
        cause the economy
        to be the way it is
              say
        everything that's gone wrong
        well   it's all their fault

you see them
          on buses
heads bobbing
          with fatigue
as they ride
          one hour or more   each way
far from home
          from some foreign place
where they left loved ones

to look for
     jobs at minimum wage
     jobs no one wants
     jobs that barely pay
          the rent
          if you live with
          just one wage earner.
     dirty jobs
     dangerous jobs
     demeaning jobs
     dull jobs
     deadend jobs
     dreary jobs
     desperate jobs
they're stealing them all.

you see them
          on buses
heads bobbing
          with fatigue
as they ride
          one hour or more   each way

continued…

mexicans and salvadoreños in los angeles
dominicans and haitians in new york
morroccans in cadiz
west africans in marseilles
turks in frankfot
west indians in london
koreans in yokahama
chinese, pakistanis, guatemalans, vietnamese, afganis, thais,
colombians, hondureños, ethiopians, filipinos, algerians
somalians, iranians, laotians, nigerians, burmese

        persons   displaced

          by
       colonialism
       imperialism
       wars
       struggles
civil   or   inspired

you see them
    on buses . . .

Sawtelle Boulevard, West L.A.

                        Los Angeles, California 1988

Vanessa and Julia were driving
south on Sawtelle one 8 a.m.,
and they passed in groups of three or more,
mexicanos, and others,
clustered on each and every corner
and on the sidewalks connecting them,
from the 7-11 on Santa Monica,
beside *loncheras* dotting the street,
and on to Tomy's restaurant on Pico.
They were dressed in Goodwill and Salvation Army clothing,
and they waited for work by day or by week.

"Look at those foreigners.
They're probably all illegals,"
Vanessa exclaimed.
"If they didn't breed like rabbits down there,
they wouldn't have to come up here.
They flood across the border
inundating us and they take jobs away
from everyone."

"Well," Julia replied, "some get a few hours work
in the Japanese nurseries lining Sawtelle.
And look at the pick-ups filled with gardening tools.
Some soon will be taken to Pacific Palisades and Beverly Hills,
where aunts and sisters are laboring as maids."

"They take factory jobs away as well,"
Vanessa snapped in anger.
"And on every construction site
you see them.
They take employment away,
from citizens born here."

                                                     continued…

"Yes, they are utilized in construction cleanup,
they're among the non-unionized.
The developer earns money that way.
And they load and unload semis
for sweatshops where sisters and cousins
are working ten hour shifts
most of the time for less
than legal minimum wage."

"They're responsible for the housing crisis too,"
Vanessa continues, eyes flashing.
"With all those aliens here
the landlords charge the rents they want
and we all have to pay the same.
Besides, they crowd in everyone they can,
play that foreign music until midnight,
and just simply ruin the neighborhoods."

"Yes, Vanessa. It is true.
The landlords charge them as much as they can,
with the threat of having them deported,
should they think to complain.
And they live from five to twenty or even more
in apartments from Sepulveda to eleventh,
and even on to Venice
—if we're talking only about the west side,
while they send all they can to widowed mothers,
wives and children if left behind,
as they most often are:
It costs less to lodge with other working men."

"Why do they come here if it's so bad?
Why don't they go back home
to Acapulco or Cancún or Puerta Vallarta,
where they can make handicrafts to sell,
or where they can staff the tourist hotels?"
Vanessa queries, unconvinced.

"They come from rural *ranchos*,
where tourists do not visit,
or from semi-serviced squatter settlements,
not on the Grey Line stops,
where floors are of earth,
and the rain leaks in,
and children seldom see,
fresh fruit or greens,
though they're grown back there
by U.S. agribusiness,
for export to east coast supermarket chains.
And I bet that's where they'd rather be,
than in what a song about them called
this cage of gold.
But they take whatever comes their way,
so their families can survive."

"We're not responsible for them,
it's not at all our fault.
Why should we bear the burden?
If the U.S. hadn't taken
California away,
Los Angeles would be just like
any other bar-filled border town.
Why don't they just
go back
to where
they belong?"

continued…

Julia didn't continue the discussion
but she hoped that just one year,
there'd be enough work in Mexico,
so these men, women and boys wouldn't have to come up here.
When the prices of clothing and lettuce doubled,
when there were no busboys and restaurants closed,
when there were no house cleaners or hotel maids
when more small businesses began to disappear,
people like Vanessa would start begging,
—if they made the connection at least—
for the Border Patrol,
to linger over coffee and donuts,
just a few hours, please.

Garments

Los Angeles, California 1988

Elena begins her ten hour shift   at dawn
leans to her double-needled   grey machine
guides   drab olive fabric   strict and straight
mental images   flash forth   unwilled   as day draws on
the green damp jungle palms   papayas   *platanos*
her brother Alejandro   four years ago
machine gunned down   beneath the trees   by men in uniform
for organizing   coffee pickers   pressing for a living wage
her father Estebán   face drawn   the night before he   disappeared
"I hope he's with   the other woman"   her mother wept
deranged   as she died   of ulcers bleeding.
There was no other woman and she knew.

Elena listens to   the hum and clink   the hum and clink
of her machine
recalls *sangudos*   swarming   arrive at dusk   suck blood
a hum punctuated   by gunshots   staccato   late at night.
Children sob   tremble   are sometimes torn apart
by land mines   planted beneath palms   papayas   *platanos*

Elena sits   in an L. A. warehouse
with *paisanas*   from Guatemala   her widowed *tía* Marta too
compañeras   *mexicanas*   *salvadoreñas*   and others
six days   each week   arrayed in rows   strict and straight
clothed   in unwanted memories   in the windowless expanse
struggling still   with aching backs   and failing sight
and mutilated finger tips.

Rosario

></p>Los Angeles, California 1986

Born on a *rancho* in Zacatecas *lejos de* Fresnillo,
one of seven children and amongst the eldest
Rosario fell in love with her Julio
at the innocent age of fourteen.
And her heart pounded against her ribcage.

Rosario begged to go to the *tiendita*
when her mother needed someone for the chore
to buy *salsa de tomate*, *arroz or* pasta
because he stood there with his brothers, near the door,
evenings after working in the corn.

Julio noticed her charming, ever present smile
her eager, polite, "*Buenas noches.*"
He began to reply in kind.
He began to dance with her at *los bailes*...
And her heart pounded against her ribcage.

One day he took her up upon *el monte*
where only the *chivas* roam
and beneath the towering *nopales*
he claimed his option as a man.
And Rosario's heart pounded against her ribcage.

Pregnant at sixteen was Rosario
and Julio took her to the Church.
But not long after the birth of Nacho
Julio left for the city of Los Angeles
crossed the desert with a *coyote*

So they could build a house of their own
on their *rancho* in Zacatecas.
perhaps even buy a cow or two
perhaps even another mule.
And Rosario's heart thudded against her ribcage.

After Julio was three years gone
Rosario too crossed the border
carried her almost four year old son
over the rocks and hills near Julian
And her heart thudded against her ribcage.

Rosario soon began to clean houses,
some in Beverly Hills,
sold tamales in the *barrio* Sunday afternoons.
But Julio had become a drunkard
and a jealous one at that
suspicious of her winning smile
and where it was directed.

So one night when he returned from the *cantinas*
while she was gathering laundry from the neighboring men
he grabbed her by her long chestnut hair
threatened to smash a bottle over her head.

Rosario pulled back when their son ran between them
as he cried "*Mamá, Papá*" and Julio hit Nacho instead.
And the sidewalk filled with Nacho's bleeding.
And his face was covered with blood.

continued…

Police came to the emergency room
questioned all assembled.
Rosario said it was done by a drunken man
who'd fought on the street with her husband
while her heart pounded against her ribcage.

Rosario never reported Julio.
Angrier he'd be when he got out of jail.
And without his earnings as a day laborer
how would they survive?
But her heart thudded against her ribcage.

Newcomer

                Los Angeles, California 1993

She watched Sagittarius pursue Scorpio and Libra
       their nightly voyage
              toward the Pacific
       waves beating
       six miles from where she lay
       on the Federal Building's
             lawn
                     after finishing her supper
       of hamburger remains
       fished from Burger King's
             garbage cans.

She watched a comet surge over Jupiter
  her now constant nighttime friend
  the meteorite hail
       like mirrors
       reflecting
  the firefly headlights
       intermittent
             on Freeway 405.

She watched the crescent moon arise
       chase Saturn
       whose planetary rings
       tilted more and more each night
             pulled the newspapers
             more tightly around her

continued...

And she wished for a fleeting moment
        but for less time that it took
        the Kopff comet
        to flare then disappear
                that she had meandered over
                to Santa Monica for
                the Salvation Army's give-away day
                last week
        (But she's been less than one month on the streets)

She turned her head and slept
        then awoke at dawn
She watched the ants
        in the damp grass
        carry crumbs from her last night's dinner
        to their sandy nest.

My Neighbor, Noreen

>   Westwood Village, 1989

Stone stairs trickle
down the two storey hillside
filled with geraniums, bromeliads, and roses,
touch the pavement below
    lined with cars
    and garbage pails
    visited by an occasional rat.

Noreen's living room window
overlooks the geraniums and bromeliads.
    While she watches the Lakers—
    she knows each player's name—
    and six talk shows a week,
    they grow.

Springtime in Los Angeles means
Noreen has passed one more year alone
    since her mother died of cancer
    nineteen years ago
    and her abusive spouse
    thankfully, walked out.

Noreen still talks about how her mother made
fried chicken on Friday afternoons
and the best cherry jello for dessert.
    I cannot relate:
    My mother always wasn't there,
    for she had left an uncivil husband too.

continued…

But Noreen still waits for her Prince Charming:
Unannouced is o.k., but she gets up late.
    She thinks perhaps she'll meet him
    if she goes to luncheon twice a week
    at the Sizzler's on Gayley Avenue
    two blocks down the street
    from the faded apartment
    where she has resided
    since arriving here from Brooklyn
    in the years Roosevelt gave fireside chats
    to admiring audiences: She was among them.

She's acquainted with all the busboys and waiters:
They banter with her and share their jokes
    bring her extra broccoli, garlic bread,
    after-dinner mints.
    But the problem is she's fifty-eight
    and none of them were even alive
    when the Dallas assassination
    was televised.

At night, after watching Colombo—
Whenever he is on—
And the channel seven news,
Noreen approaches her window
    opens the shade,
    adjusts her glasses,
    and with a smile
    she tries to see
    the young couple from Apartment 3,
    kissing on the stairs.

Port City Women

Butterflies

Belawan, Indonesia 1979

In a port town called Belawan
south side of Indonesia
my then husband and I
on my first trip as *messpike*
with most of the crew as well
went to a quarter
walled by wooden stakes
wound with barbed wire

filled with a number
of immense shabby structures
one fronted by a ramada
sheltering small tables and rattan chairs
and a kneeling aged billy goat
front legs twisted and broken.

We stopped for a beer
and then walked on
past rows and rows of thatched constructions.
In each an earthen floored barroom
an array of women
who alighted like butterflies
quivering and silent
at the tables and benches
we went in and occupied.

Young women, pretty women
long dark hair and blossom mouths
they sat in silence smiling
waited to be offered a drink
for which they earned
a few *rupiahs*
or to dance with whomever neared them.

continued…

One spoke to me, a small slight girl
in halting English mixed with Dutch.
"Don't think me bad," she plead,
"I worked in the rice fields since I was nine,
my father had no land
without a dowry who would want me?"

She paused a moment before she said,
"I came to work here four years ago
when I was seventeen—older than most.
I may have four more years to go
before I have to leave."

She motioned toward another woman
at a nearby table.
"My cousin was the first one here
from our village two days walk away.
She's twenty-five and soon she'll be heading
to the Djakarta streets.
At least here we have protection."

Not knowing what to say
and still not understanding
I answered lightly:
"What's wrong with dancing and drinking?"
She looked at me in surprise
(perhaps she was astounded)
then smiled, looked toward the outside,
and replied: "Sometimes we get tired you know."

Later that night, after several drinks,
I asked her where the restrooms were.
"I'll take you," she said and led me
to the back of the barroom
through faded batik curtains
and I saw on either side
rows of rooms, each filled by a bed,
a small table flaking paint
adorned by tin cans holding melting candles
a dress or two or blouse or pants
hung from a nail in each nook of planks.

Through the gauntlet of rooms
some filled with coupling
I walked to the rear exit
where she showed me the empty lot
the open air bathroom for residents.

She waited while I wet the earth
then took me back through the long hallway
to the drunk filled palm thatched barroom
where I sat
not speaking
not having known.

Seamen's Girls

Manila, Philipines 1979

Cardboard shacks roofed with tarpaulin
children wearing tee-shirts nothing more
they beg for coins or gum or cigarettes.
Twisting walkways filled with trash
rusting cans and gnawing rats.

Estellie emerges from the one room structure
shared with widowed mother,
five younger sisters and brothers
and a ten year old boy they found last year
abandoned on the garbage dump.

Wearing high heels, black stockings, red lipstick,
eye shadow, mascara and liner—her work uniform
Estellie picks her way past groups of children
through the twisting pathways filled with trash
rusting cans and packs of rats

until she comes to the crumbling sidewalk
makes her way past rows of taverns
turns left to the Red Lion Inn
where fourteen other women
sit at booths or beside the bar.

It is only six: the seamen still at dinner
back on their ships, in port or at anchor:
They'll start trickling in between seven and ten
some for a drink before they move on
some to stay, flirt and indulge

some of the barmaids at a nearby hotel
or even take them back on board
give them a few tins of sardines
a loaf of bread or a kilo of cheese
besides their usual charge.

Estellie walks to the small corner booth
where Betty and Veronica are seated
painting their nails the newest style
pearl with red or purple half moons or diamonds
something to do while waiting.

Estellie's brought her nail polish remover
and the almost empty bottle of coral lacquer
one of the boys who hangs on the corner
found in a garbage pail and gave her.

"Betty, can you be so kind to do my nails like yours?"
And Betty bends to the task, while the three sit
wait for the men to tumble in
wait for their work to begin.

They'll listen to the juke box music
perhaps make some money from drinks
perhaps go to the nearby hotel
or visit a ship to stay overnight,
before they return to the twisting paths
strewn with trash, overrun by rats,
home to their cardboard shacks.

Migrant Women

>   Cristobal Colón, Panama 1980

One night when our ship was anchored in the Panama Canal
with no hope of moving through the locks until the following day
the captain arranged for us to go ashore.

Three of us from the M/S Tirana
went together and roamed about
streets filled with vendors selling handmade things:
From a bent and grey-haired woman
we bought knitted scarfs and sailor's caps.

We went to one bar, then to another,
we sat at a table with a woman called Carmela
being hugged by a deckhand named Bjørn.
Knowing coupling would come later, she drank Coca Cola.
I asked her about Panama, she told me about Colombia.

"I'm from a rural village where
men pass through to work on the coffee farms
and I fell in love with a man named Velorio.
He left me with a baby daughter before he went away
perhaps to a wife he hadn't mentioned
perhaps like others he was disappeared.

"My father was murdered when I was small.
I have no brothers living.
So six months each year I come here
and send back money that I earn
to support my mother and Angelina.

"I live with them for the other six months
sometimes work in the coffee fields.
My *comadre* Paula is just like me
though she has three babies, not just one,
so we came to an arrangement.

"While I am here she's in the village,
and she comes to take my place
when I return to be with my Angelina,
watch her grow and buy her dresses.
Most of us here are *ilegales*.
We cross the border in the night
to come here where there are dollars."

Then Carmela and Bjørn
climbed to a room upstairs
just a few minutes before
a young girl called Rocio
sat beside an engine boy named Tør.

We left and walked through brightly lit streets
lined with bars and vendors.
We headed toward the water taxi
that would take us back to the ship again
for tomorrow early we'd be leaving.

And ships go through the Panama Canal
and ships wait anchored to enter the locks
while in Cristobal Colón and Balboa
women wait for passing crews to land
to earn some money then be abandoned.

Three Dollars

> Miami, Florida 1972

Far from Montego Bay or Kingston
Evie lived in a thirty-shack settlement
where there was one bar selling sugar cane rum
where people eat chick peas, pasta and rice
an occasional egg, never a chop.

Evie was fragile and childlike
and only aged thirteen
when a man wandered over
said he'd give her three dollars
if she'd let him do things to her.

She had never seen three dollars
all at one single time
so she agreed and kept smiling:
She had heard whimpers in the shacks at night.
She had seen stray dogs line up.

By fifteen Evie was pregnant
she wasn't sure to whom.
Two years after her daughter's birth
she went to Miami to work in a bar
dollars stuffed into her bikini, into her bra.

She smokes *ganja* to get through the evening
she smokes *ganja* to get through the night
smiles to the old men, smiles to the young
thinks of her daughter coming on twelve
sends money for her schooling.

Sometimes Evie prays
though she is not a believer
that the three dollars allowance she sends
for each and every day
will keep her daughter from following her way.

A Dollar a Drink

                    Singapore 1974

           I

Singapore port area 1974
small shops: fruit, greens, rice displayed.
Buddhist monks in saffron robes
extend wooded begging bowls.
Rows and rows of seaman's bars.
One: the Paradise Lounge.

Inside: Bulgarians and Greeks,
Japanese, Dutch and Swedes.
And there as well: Pettri, a Finnish sailor,
outsider among our Norwegian crew,
quiet, serious, twenty-five.

Pettri has a woman there
whom he visits each time he comes to port.
A Malay girl named Myrna
who earns a Singapore dollar a drink.

"I came to be a school teacher," she tells me.
"That's what my parents think I am.
But there are no jobs for one like me,
I'm not Chinese
and I could never get to college."

"I've worked here more that three years now.
I met Pettri soon after I started.
I stay with him when his ship is in
about every four months or so
then return here when he sails away,
until he's back again.
I'd be willing to work in a store or a factory.

My husband would not have to support me.
I wish it could be Pettri."

Pettri kept on seeing Myrna,
then one day he jumped ship.
He didn't have the papers to marry her:
Couldn't find work, was deported,
and banned from merchant fleets.

Now he's employed in a beer packing plant
in Oslo and he's drunk most of the time.
He thinks of Myrna but cannot get back.
He's illegal in Norway, jobless in Finland
and he's afraid to write.

II

Years later Myrna still sat at the Paradise Lounge
still drank cold tea in liquor glasses
watched the door night after night
hoped against hope Pettri might walk in
before she left, escorted.

If they hadn't bulldozed
that part of Singapore down
cemented it over, built tourist hotels
she'd still be waiting at the Paradise Lounge.

Pettri's more than fifty now
he never has been married. Sometimes he looks
at the address Myrna once gave him
tucked into his pocket, always with him.
though he knows its useless now.

Decatur Street

New Orleans, Louisiana 2002

More than a decade has passed since I left the sea
but I remember Decatur Street
lined with dimly lit bars, rhythmic sounds extruding, like the breasts
    of the women who stood in the doorways.
A purple fronted restaurant, opened by some crewmen who had
jumped ship,
    serving grape leaves and rice, black olives and feta cheese.
A Cantonese take out place that also delivered
    to several cheap hotels, renting rooms by hour or week.
The bars filled with seamen, Norwegians, Israelis, mostly Greeks
  listening to bazouki jukebox music
  waited on by bargirls who accompanied them
      to rooms upstairs
      or down the street
      or back to their cabins
after watching deck hands and engine boys attached by white
handkerchiefs
    step and hop around thick glasses of crystal ouzo
    as one of each partnered pair, hand behind his back,
    stooped and picked up the libation from the floor
    with his teeth: their entertainment while in port
    recreating the village life they said they missed
in a bar they'd return to each trip, acting out more or less the same
script.

I remember Decatur Street
when it was populated by women of mixed and many colors
migrating into New Orleans from swamplands and bayous and
Baton Rouge,
who drank with men just in from Bahía or Hong Kong
heading soon to Rotterdam or back to Yokohama.
They cared for one another, sitting at tables in twos or threes,
sharing taxis back from the docks,

presiding over barroom festivities.
And once a belly dancer came:
Wearing scarlet veils she dipped and swirled
for money thrown into an upturned hat, that filled twice to its brim.
And the night bartender was a dark skinned handsome male
      who stowed away his tips to finance his desired sex-change
      then years later earned a dollar a drink
      and walked the streets
      and went to ships
and defended her sisters from drunks and thieves.

A decade passes after I leave the sea
and I take some friends to show them a part of my past
where I'd worked some weeks, serving drinks, while waiting to sign on a ship,
where some hands and I had spent some time when we sailed back from
      Singapore, Bangkok and Penang,
to down some beer or rum and coke, and watch the dancers twirling.
Homogenized, hygenitized, I found that vacated street
encroached upon by tourists' restaurants, sanitized and selling pricey
      jambalaya, three tables filled of twenty,
      untenanted by rural migrant women
      emptied of seafaring crews,
      absent the port party atmosphere
      gone the seamen's haunts.
"The girls have moved eight blocks up," a white-shirted waiter responded
to my distressed remark about unexpected changes.

Perhaps some day I'll go
the eight blocks up from Decatur Street
to see where all the boys hang out now,
and if Gloria and Rosie are still working
and if bazouki music still fills the air while dancers leap and whirl

continued…

            but only if I sign on another line
            and sail again up the Mississippi,
            and lose some age, because now I'm too old,
            to roam the world once more,
            haunting ports and bars and painting decks
            and riding out the stormy seas.
    I first came here forty years ago, but now I'm pushing sixty.

Elsewhere's Women

"La Vibora"

>Playa de Panama, Costa Rica 1982

No one gossips about "La Vibora":
No one knows how many men she's had.
She's borne living children to not a one.
They fear her temper and they fear her blade
and besides, she's a witch, she says.

She drinks with the men
carries a knife like them
has been known to pull it
at the near midnight fights
leave a nick or a slash
to remember her by.

"La Vibora" may put a dead snake
outside your door or on a stake
or fill a bottle with your hair and nails
then something happens you wish would not:
Your husband gets another woman.
Your youngest baby dies.

"La Vibora" is feared and envied
by women who sit patiently
in the unlit shacks, awaiting the return
of drunken husbands from the bars
where "La Vibora" wields her powers.

Catch

                    Playa de Panama, Costa Rica 1982

In Costa Rica
in palm fragrant places
out in the countryside
there's not much work.
Men sleep with women
then move on
or marry or unite
then have another wife
on the side
and children with maybe three.

Playa de Panama,
jungle enclave on edge of bay:
Concha with her baby is unwed
and her father's outdoor café
on cream-colored beach
unspoiled by tourists
except for a handful
on alternate weekends
barely helps them get by.
They collect mussels and mangos
and wild *quadrados*
and hearts of palm to eat.

A small settlement
maybe twenty houses
each one to three rooms
washing water comes from the stream
light comes from the sun.

Two other women about Concha's age
were abandoned by men
who wandered elsewhere
in search of a wage:
There's nothing to earn in the jungle
except fruits of papaya and *platano*.

There are some painted fishing boats
with crews of ten
that mine the Pacific
give jobs to some men:
No women venture on board;
they would be gang-raped if they dared.

So Concha and her two *amigas*
borrow an old rowboat
or repossess it from where it sits
abandoned on the shore.
They caulk the holes then take pull it to the sea;
They cast out lines and set lobster traps
in the shade of craggy rocks.

Then they carry their catch
in baskets and pails
to the tourist hotel
three or four winding miles
down the rutted yellow road:
Rain pouring down or hot and humid
they walk there and back.
They decided it was better all around
to extend some lines and set some traps
and let the *macho*s go on their way.

Turquoise and Silver, 1999

Navajo turquoise
vast dust-filled reservation
old woman sits beside
sparsely traveled road
walked three miles
from her unserviced hogan
to sell silver and turquoise
alongside the highway.
And her Vietnam Veteran son
uses his spare pension
to drink day after day
in Gallup, New Mexico bars.

Ojibwa women in Vancouver bar
I lend her my Navajo bracelet
so she can cross the border to find
her husband in Arizona
she who has no birth certificate
born in a northeastern hamlet.
The INS can't tell one tribe from another
they let Indians cross with little proof.
The bracelet is her document
she'll pass as a Navajo woman:
she bears their turquoise and silver.

The Witch

> Penns Creek, Pennsylvania 1951

My next to last stepmother
considered herself a folk-healer
and to impress my father
once when I tossed with fever
and snowdrifts filled the highway
and we didn't have much money anyway
sent someone to fetch leeches from the creek
then put them on my belly
to suck my blood away.

My skin curled beneath their bloated bodies
the stench of dried blood filled the air:
I wept in fear, stomach churning
was told to keep quiet, it was for my own good.

Why didn't my stepmother, healer as she claimed to be
not send someone a few yards up the mountain
to gather some sassafras leaves?
Because it was a widespread practice
I later came to know
to brew tea from the sassafras
to cure the winters' fevers.

Faded Purple

                Bayport, Long Island 1975

Purple irises jutted forth
punctuated with jonquil yellow
in my grandmother's garden.
Purple pansies laced with black
clustered in a bed
outside the screened-in porch
where canaries sang in well-kept cages.
She had me crack the pansy pods
scatter seeds so more would grow
while her thinning, arthritic body
bent to pull the weeds.

My grandmother's pride was her garden then
and she groomed it when she could:
Cut back the pink briar roses
to tame the bushes' rambling growth;
mold grape vines to their trestles
then displayed their red purple issue
on the kitchen table where we dined;
pruned the bridal wreath in fall;
shaped the rhododendron trees;
cultivated purple hyacinths
interspersed with white, in spring:
in her younger days.

In the oblong sitting room
where in autumn the family sat
to watch hurricanes torment the sky
or in winter, the snowflakes tumbling,
were planters with African violets,
purple too.

And sometimes we children brought her
Bells of Ireland from nearby fields
which she displayed on the window sills
in small ceramic vases,
now cracked and gone.

Then she moved to a smaller house
after my grandfather died
where untrimmed branches of lilac trees
scratched against the eastern wall
and lilies of the valley
tangled with Queen Anne's lace,
wild daiseys and dandelion puffs,
while grandmother sat at the window
looking outward all afternoon
as her purple haltingly faded
first to lavender
then into the grey beyond.

Clash

Lewisburg, Pennsylvania 1993

"You wouldn't have let me work at sea, or live in the jungle in Costa Rica, or in a *colonia popular* in Mexicali, or a *rancho* in Jalisco, if you had brought me up, would you mother?" I asked after not having seen her for twenty-five years.

"No, you would have had a different life. Though we're proud Carl and I that you got your Ph.D. How could you have lived in the jungle anyway and amidst such poverty? I would only stay at hotels with room service and a spa." (She was brought up in a small house by the river by an aunt who worked in a garment factory).

"I wanted to see the world—not only the good things but also the sad things, and the many different things, though many are the same."

"But scrubbing floors on a ship, washing dishes, serving food—isn't that sort of, something you'd rather have someone else do—perhaps if you went on a cruise?"

"I saw thirty-seven countries mother, from Indonesia to Qatar, from Australia to Italy, from Singapore to Canada, port cities like Rotterdam, Dubai, Manila and Penang. I learned more than from any of my degrees."

"How could you stand the misery you saw? Carl once wanted to build dams and bridges in those countries—the underdeveloped ones. But I dissuaded him of that, I like my luxuries. I've only been out of the country once, and to tell the truth I prefer the Hiltons here. I don't understand why you don't want a home, instead of wandering here and there."

Then she walked to the oven and pulled out a pie
made from cherries picked in their backyard.
I had never learned to bake.

Fragments
Of an Autobiography

Reading Allen Ginsberg's Reading Bai Juyi-I

I was a stranger in a neighboring country
and I've seen *ranchos, pueblos,* cities.
Now I am living in Los Cabos, days
on my terrace with its views of the sea
a commodity here mainly for expatriates.
Thousands live in squatter settlements
awake at dawn to fill their buckets
wash dishes, clothes, wet down dirt floors,
while I sleep late, smoke too much,
drink coffee, snooze to dream of
the absent, whether alive or dead
in flashy video colored format.
I can go to the seaside or marina restaurants
but today I prefer my windowed kitchen, my
aloneness. I don't have to rise to
sell fake silver, wooden statues, beaded bracelets
on the beach in Cabo San Lucas, like the
myriad vendors in their white uniforms.
Don't have to scurry to the luxury hotels
to mop their halls and rooms and plazas, or
search for coins to pay the water truck—I am moneyed
my research may have done some good
at least nothing bad, though I may never know.
still I feel guilty that I've not done more.
True I wrote about the impoverished
the brickmakers, the garbage pickers, the immigrants
sometimes about love and loss and men and women.
But my own practice has been in comfort
my donations inadequate, my activism intermittent.
I am lazy, take advantage of income
received recently for no work I have done. But
I'll stay in bed and read articles and poetry,
prepare for my next written projects.

continued…

If there is reincarnation
I may be punished for doing so little
reborn in a squatter settlement
with my hands grubbing through the garbage dump
for clothes, kitchen utensils, and magazines.

Fleeting Honeymoon

Confusion torments my mind
inundates my thoughts
perforates my emotions
confounds my feelings.

How could he, so sweet, so loving
so charming most of the time
turn on me like a wild thing
punch me in the nose and forehead

shout "Someday I'll kill you"?
Gives as his reasons I haven't washed the floors
I spend too much time at my desk
write stuff that will never change the world

read books no one cares about
that he's threatened to incinerate
then comes all smiles and lovingly
and wonders why I didn't want

to clasp his body against mine.
Yet, now alone, I play with the idea
when I remember his kindnesses:
Sometimes he brought me coffee in the mornings;

sometimes he made the midday meal.
It was most often he who fed and pet the cats
but sometimes also turned on them
threw stones at one shy male

who would not approach at his bidding
who attacked, immediately ran away
confounded, confused, astounded.
He never did come back.

Drugs

I look   carefully
at my face   in the mirror
over the cream-colored chest of drawers
I bought when I first loved him.
inspect   how a shadow
deletes   lights of the iris
inspect   how the turn of my mouth
shows disillusion.

Disappointment is reflected in
more recent photographs
disappointment not there
three or four years ago.

I turn away
try to find solace in Neitzche's words:
"That which doesn't kill me
                        will make me stronger"

Loving him almost killed me
caused shadows to enter my eyes
pulled my lips toward a downward angle
made me distrust almost everyone

made me hate the *narcotraficantes*
whose offerings
turned him from being
the light of my soul
into a lingering   searing   crippling
                               regret.

Monadic Me

Unrelenting solitude, monadic isolation
is my freedom, and my burden.
I slumber when I wish, arise the hour I choose,
work the hours that suit me (though that's sometimes 10 a day),
depart to other cities, countries, continents
constrained only by my bank account.
I am the sole architect of my decisions
the only engineer of my plans
the lone interpreter of my autobiographical text
the unhampered administrator of my free time.
No one hinders my mobility.
No one criticizes my opinions.
No one intervenes in my routines.

But I sleep alone in a big wide bed
with no one to ratify my California mornings,
Jalisco summers, Dublin autumns, Mexicali springs,
nor co-author anywhere.
No being beckons me to the world of his imaginations.
No beloved lifts me from inertia.
No companion adds dimensions to my thoughts.
No lover accompanies me through joys and sorrowings
or multiplies my motivations.
Relentless solitude, monadic isolation
is my freedom, and my burden.

Love At First Glance

I

You could not have been genetically encoded from
germoplasm of any man or woman I have seen in my travels:
From the almost epicanthic fold of your eyelid
to the smooth proportions of your back, thigh, calf
you embody the imagination of an artist
whose fame will endure for having sculpted you.

II

You didn't turn to look at me looking at you:
I might have been incinerated by your glance
I might have disintegrated into atomic particles
by the fissioning beauty of your eyes.

Upon Reading Pope's Reading Of Horace's Ode I

Again! Once more your searching glances filled with silent pleas!
They threaten my long sought equilibrium, my acquiesences,
achieved by smothering, smashing, de-anchoring, annihilating
all hope we'd occupy a shared space-time continuum.

The year you were birthed I initially embarked
upon my seafaring days, moved intermittently from port to port
on sailing ships immersed in undulating, rough fluidities
while I contemplated diversity, interrogated geographies.

Decades had past when I eventually intruded
deep inland to the rainless valley where I wished to rest
where you first sought, then abandoned me
incited in your flight by ridicule of my greater age.

So I too deserted, cast off from the place we both called home
continued my wandering, explored regions still unknown,
catabolism setting in, as I repressed my desperation
elicited by tormented recognition that my harbor wasn't yours.

Now graying, wrinkled, inundated, I return once more
to the unpaved streets of your *colonia,* and hear you claim:
"It doesn't matter anymore. Your age I mean."
But this time I beg: "Free me! Seek elsewhere your guiding
constellations:

"Turn, love, to those night long dusty dances on unplotted land,
beneath Mexicali's arid skies where *rancheras* effervesce.
Go. Embrace with impassioned fervor Ernestina or Erlinda:
She who is to navigate your still unchartered course

continued…

"bear your children my infertile womb refuses
knead your *tortillas de harina* in the early morning hours
weather your excursions through Rumarosa mountains
your sporadic forays to Pacific shores. I am too old.

"For the year your were born, I bore your present age
and crisscrossed several oceans to sundry foreign coasts
but now my future is congealed into flat predictability
while yours, still malleable, unsolidified, is the rising tide."

So You Want Me Back?

You brutalized my nights for three long years
using a blunt scalpel to carve away pieces of my liver
without even the anesthetic of knowing when you'd be home,
until punished, I wanted no one anymore, not even you.

Then you leave me, in the chest of drawers beside our bed
where you neglect to sleep too often
a Silvio Rodriguez cassette stopped at "Te Amaré."

You *will* love me? How long must I wait
stabbed by your absences, perforated by doubts and empty hours?
Do you think now I will turn to you once more,
so you can callously cut more scraps from my soul
as I wait night after night for your return from the *cantinas*?
Or wherever else you go?

You will have to do more than leave me
obtuse messages of love in bureau drawers,
messages you can pretend were not for me should I displease you:
You will have to suture wounds from lonely nights and days
with the totality of your life force, endless embraces;
You will have to use a silver needle held in your teeth
to sew iron threads of promises never to be bent or broken;
You will have to sanitize each festering sour
with *spoken* words of adoration day after day;
You will have to debraid the suppurating scars
you left encrusted on my aorta and my brain
with your constant presence before my starving eyes.

En Fin

How strange. I woke up yesterday
not loving you anymore, at least not like before,
not missing you like a piece of amputated self,
I who once thought this passion, this emotion
You wound around me like a galvanic coil
would last for years, though several lives
at least until post-Apocalypse.

I do admit that when I remember you as you were:
Your shynesses, your kindnesses,
the glances from the corner of your eye
I feel a twinge in vital organs
and not so vital ones as well.
Yes, still.

But you have changed
become another configuration
another being, estranged from any
connection with your former self,
severed from me, indifferent to my longings.

My feelings, thankfully, have been annulled;
today I no longer suffer about your fickleness,
your sudden arrivals and prolonged departures,
necessary, you seem to think,
to prove your independence, your *hombría*.

Sad to know I'll never find some idealized eternal love;
Glad to know the magnet's lines are broken
and I am free to move outside your field of force
liberated at last, a monadic particle, though that's not new:
There was no symmetry, no dyadic bond between us.

It happened yesterday while you were gone.
I was unfaithful to you with another man
         in my mind.
His hair is shorter, and unwaved,
he outweighs you by several pounds.
He entered to draw me from you voltaic range
         in a dream.
I should send him a thank you note
on fragile paper lined with gold
but I don't know his name.

After He Moved On

Whirlwinds whirl and rush and damage
I fall into the center of the raging storm
friction burns upon my being, leaving scars:
Missing you is hurting me, this lifeway is over
another path must be embraced
blocking out, cementing closed, a world withdrawn.

Whirlwind, roulette wheel, where will I land?
You de-anchored me from what I knew not were flimsy dreams
    of where and what and how to build with you.
You ripped me asunder, brutalizingly, like a crowbar
    speared into a brick wall.

Please come back I beg your photographs
But if you do
are not the foundations cracked and failing
    and what can we construct with such unsteady gear?
    The whirlwind has reached within our us.

But I'll miss you
    miss the world we could have erected
    with our interpenetrating thinkings and desirings
    our interdependencies, your specific, my specific, permeabilities
    insulating us from raging cyclonic storms.

And I'll miss you long and even after
another engineering feat is performed upon my destiny
by an architect as yet unknown.
And I'll cry for my dislodged foothold in the life
    we never will create, the unknown I'll never know
    the existence you could have spun around my nodal self
    our nodal selves
    with the web of your loved being
    with my web entwined
    to anchor and protect me from the whirlwind.

Cross-Border Love Canals

Pussy willows and cat-o-nine tails
        dragon flies, love bugs, and butterflies
                clustered beside the boat canals
                        that meandered into Bayport's Bay.
I passed them on my chestnut mare
        brought grey knobbed willow branches to adorn
                the antique Chinese vases
                        in my widowed grandmother's summer house
visited by cardinals, blue jays and wild canaries
        and myriad fireflies illuminated
                the lilacs and wisteria
                        after dusk.

Tule reeds, miniature bamboo,
        mesquite and eucalyptus trees
                punctuated the sides of Mexicali's irrigation canals
                        which surged forth from the Río Colorado.
He lived on the banks of the brickyard's canal
        brought turtles, frogs, and catfish
                to share with his four younger brothers
                        in their one room abode
visited by robins, crows, sparrows and wild ducks
        and multitudinous mosquitos tortured
                the dry, hot desert
                      after sunset.

Flora and fauna appear
        in the stories we tell one another:
                My Bayport Bay
                      eventually streamed into
        his canals, rivers, and lagoons:
        We now share accounts
                of the byways we wander,
                      the fish we see jumping,

continued…

  the birds we see winging
     the wry, funny insects,
        chipmunks and geckos
           that are his pets.
The three thousand miles that once ran on between us
     divided by an international boundaryline
        —and other separations—
           have now intertwined.

Like Widowhood

I sit in my brown padded high backed chair
in my book-filled bedroom-sitting room
drinking Presidente on the rocks in a blue tinted glass
tuning in cable channels I don't watch
occasionally calling someone then wishing I hadn't
watching the geraniums grow

thinking of what I'll never have with you again
beer and *clamato* on the terrace, or cabernet sauvignon,
followed by sirloin or *huachinango*
Rosarito beaches on horseback at sunset
Los Cabos rock formations at dawn
San Felipe, Chichen Itza, Cancún.

thinking of all the things we would have done
visit a *rancho* in Sinaloa or Michoácan,
go to Mérida, Palenque, Monte Albán.
and if I let my imagination go: The Carnival in Río or Bahía,
the Dublin horse show in August, London in September,
rodeos in Arizona all year round,
Maui, Alaska, Long Island sound.

Meanwhile
I wallow in my aloneness
refuse significant interactions, especially with males
don't go out to anywhere too long
as if immersing myself in some magical ritual
enhancing my my pain, my solitude, my missing you:
As though my abstentions would
        resurrect your presence
        annul your absence
        bring you back.

Alone On the Shore

I

The muted steel gray waves fringed with frothy white foam
I am beside them now, not upon them, as in the years when I sailed
the sea.

The twilight color spectrum illuminates the rushing water,
and I recall the past, the past to which I never can return:
Uprooted seaweed wanders never to take root in the same place
again.

My present is aloneness, as I walk down the solitary shore
banked by pastel-hued sand flowers numerous as my memories:
But there are no ships in sight.

What I see has no meaning, for no one seas it with me,
no one knows if Bergsen's trees are falling in the forest,
there is no other witness
no one knows if yellow buttercup images adorning sand dunes exist
there is no other witness
thus my visions have no meaning.

For a moment I will sit
look out to the ever flowing ocean
focus on the tiny grains of sand
contemplate my future.

But the dimensions of my future are unknown
for I am free in ways others are not free:
Infinite possibilities confront, confound me
as numerous as the multitudinous grains of sand which surround me.

I am free because I have no one with whom to agree
about where we are going, or to stop me from leaving,
I can roam wherever I wish to roam
with my degrees that authorize me to conduct research anywhere
on the human condition.

But I need the limiting influence you exerted
to make myself complete
to tame the infinity that bludgeons me like the eye of a tornado
into which I may fall, and disappear.
I need someone to constrain me
in my adaptation to his existential being
to ten or twenty or a hundred possibilities
a number more easily chosen from.

II

The cresting waves
the shifting sand
the closing flowers
the twilight sky
I see them, smell them, hear them, know them—alone.

You no longer share them with me
or if you do, I do not know.
Although most would consider these inspiring el elements
of natural wondrous things
their occurrence leaves me empty, joyless, sad and lonely

because I will never be able to say again
"Remember when we saw . . ."

You Were My River

river washing
over river polished stones
over river cut clay
over river cut loam

river rushing
through mountains
through hills
through plains

river rushing
filling lakes
capturing steams
performing cascades

you fertilized my valleys
you led me down high mountains
you angled through my rolling hills
you inundated my meadows

Past Pleasures

I have reached an age when I am alone
and most ex-husbands and ex-lovers are dead and gone
and though most irritated me at one time or another
(which is why they were exes)
I remember some with nostalgia
I remember some with pleasure.

Jackie, my only son's father, with his yellow curls
really the first man who ever loved me
taught me how to sleep my head on his chest
embraced after our love making
(though our first time was beneath some bushes
and I remember the ant bites best).

Sam, so serious about psychology and poetry
constantly pushing back his glasses or forelock
wanted to read me Frannie and Zooey (which I found dull)
took me for my first trip half across the country
to New Orleans, cause of our separation
(He wanted to go on to San Francisco, I wanted to stay).

Leif, who defined himself through his job
in the Norwegian merchant marine,
which was my employer too
I accompanied him over at least five seas
stopping in many ports we drank in honky tonks and luxury restaurants
(but my job became redundant and he sailed on).

continued…

Others that meandered through my life
left indelible marks on my autobiography
taught me different points of view
(learned some new ones from me too)
we shared a world not repeatable
Long Island to California, Norway to Mexico
Saudi Arabia to Costa Rica, B.C. to D.C.

My last love, my saddest love
was all wrapped up in one man many years younger
who always held my hand, at least in the beginning.
As I grew older he loved me less
I should have prophesized such I guess
but six years his dark wavy hair tickled my shoulder, chin and breast
as we held each other close in the middle of our Queen sized
wooden bed.

Upon Reaching Sixty

Well I'm not sure I want to go out with you Mr. Jones
not with your poorly veiled intentions of moving in
I get up when I want, I chomp what I chomp
Sometimes I have lunch at four and dinner at ten
I might want to take off for Hawaii
with my ex-mother-in-law (though not her son)
or fly to Ballinasloe's horse sale and show visited by numerous men.

I might want to sit all day at my desk or in bed
write poetry, essays, letters or stories
read on mercantilism or machismo or mammals
while not being bothered by anyone else's routines.
You can come now and then to adjust my twidget
or screw in the widget on my kitchen sink
but I'm tired of a lifetime of. . . well, you make the list

I'm happy as I am and do not need to add
another author to the bookshelf that I am.
Enough men have trampled through my den
so I have enough failed romance to write about.
You can come if you want to fiddle with my hot water heater
or twiddle my fan belt or carburetor.

You can stick your programs in my computer
fool around with my fax machine and printer
Or strip the old wallpaper off of my walls
but I'm not sure I want to go out with you Mr. Jones
with all that implies: A set time for dinner, a set time for lunch
having to please, having to tease, having to implore
another husband or lover to perform each chore:
I get up when I want, I chomp what I chomp

Elsewhere's Other Autumns

Autumn in Los Cabos does not herald
purple fox grapes growing on the edges of the pined forest biome,
     eventually eclipsed
by ice-shrouded shoulders of the tarmac highway
     I'd run and slide upon
     To see whether Ned or Van or I could glide the furthest,
without falling of course,
or snow-covered corn-propagating hills, the stalks plowed under
since September,
     where I'd plunge downward on the aged rusting sled
inherited from my step-mother's daughter Joan,
     married and with a child by then,
     (her son died in a car accident during a blizzard when he was
twenty-three),
     wearing my hand-me-down blue jacket and an orange scarf
around my ears,
     trying to avoid the barbed wire fence at bottom,
     which I managed all but once as you can see if you come
close enough,
     by the minute horizontal scar beneath my left eye,
Eearned when I was racing Junior, not three feet away, who
got a nearby barb in his forehead,
     and bled all the way home, crying
     even though neither of us had won: we both hit the wire
     at the same time;
or waiting with toes and fingers burning from the chill through
worn-down boots and wrinkling socks and red knitted woolen
mittens, gifts of distant relatives,
     listening for the chain-covered tires of the yellow bus
coming round the bend,
     after picking up schoolmates from cabins by the rumbling
rock-strewn creek,
     to take us to Mifflinburg's new primary school, the first with
six rooms, not just one,
in the years when I was very young.

Autumn in Los Cabos does not anticipate
riding bicycles through the slush
one cousin on the handlebars, another on the stainless steel seat my grandmother wired
    on the bent back fender with an old clothes hanger,
    so I could haul another offspring of my aunt's, or groceries home from Shand's,
    and maybe cut through the mapled woods,
    splattering mud to either side of the sunken slender footpath,
        deepening and widening with each year's use,
    to deposit Doug and Larry at the elementary school, three streets beyond on
        the other side, and return two blocks again
    to the red brick high school building where we played hockey and the hundred yard dash,
    beside the tennis courts after three o'clock's last classes;
nor watching the angry, lead-colored spume-topped torrents while standing in front of the Nun's retreat,
    as they disgorged the opaque lifeless shells of horseshoe crabs,
    death-bleached like Chinese mourning clothes from their spring's dark walnut brownness;
    while hoping that Michael and Linda could get away to join us there,
by Bayport's bay,
    when I was in my teens.

Autumn in Los Cabos does not inspire
fear of another Pacific crossing from Yokahama to Takoma
in cargo ships filled with automobiles
    when the chains holding them in place
    break from the violence of the waves
and glasses fall shattering to the floor
    on the upper decks where the officers live and drink

continued…

cutting hands which clean the dark blue rugs
       and rope thrashing furniture to hooks screwed
in light tan walls,
       placed there to render stationary sea-animated chairs and
tables and other wood and metal fabrications,
       by experienced ship's fitters since retired from Norway's
merchant marine,
       as I did in my twenties.

Autumn in Los Cabos does not presage
the arrival of soaking evening rains,
the explosive germination of papaya trees,
the shudderings and chirping protests of monkeys huddling
       close beneath banana leaves,
puddles forming underneath the rotting wood-planked roofs
       and dampening home-sewn grass-filled mattresses
           converting dirt floors into mire and beds into a punishment
cutting Playa Panama in half
       as the stream where women launder clothes
       becomes a raging torment innundating
       the winding unpaved road
       the foot bridge washed away:
A thumping of water followed by assaults of Anopheles,
       that species which injects malaria plasmodia
       into human blood,
       who gorged themselves upon my serum
       but left me uninfected,
       in my thirty-sixth to seventh year.

Autumn in Los Cabos means
cook-outs fired by carbon chunks
       on balconies or in back yards,
       reminding me of wood fueled stoves where we daily
       prepared our rice and beans (and pigeons massacred by

sportsmen visiting from Montana)
>	for lack of gas or microwaves
>	six hours from San José in Costa Rica.

Autumn in Los Cabos is not
>	the piping horn of the water truck,
>	tapping hammers fixing roofs and walls,
>	an aged man peddling blankets door to door,
>	the ice-cream vendor's hand rung bell,
>	the woman hawking shirts picked from the dump,
>	the young wife with cactus leaves for sale,

or the Saturday dances where clinging couples
>	filteringly viewed through dusty puffings skyward bound,
>	erupting from the grounded footsteps of those frontier youth
>	who work as brickmakers, masons, garbage gatherers,
>	peddlers

and domestic servants in Baja California's capital city,
where I loved so many yet too few,
and one haunting man-child named Alberto,
>	not very long ago.

Autumn in Los Cabos means one autumn more alone
in monadic isolation, in a city where your closest friends
live farther away than Mifflinburg R.D. #1 from Penns Creek in the next door county,
>	or Bayport's park from Bluepoint's beach,
>	or my Mexicali colonia from the neighboring one.

You can walk there in less time than it takes to drive from here
>	to Cabo San Lucas, you know.

I wonder what Junior, who became a marine in 1962 right after turning age eighteen, I have no news since then,
>	and "skinny" Ned and "shorty" Van are doing now,

continued…

And Michael who was incarcerated in a German concentration camp for one full year before he reached birthday eleven
exiting with no unshattered tooth:
  The Michael who told us in eighth grade that he wanted to study
    theoretical physics at Stanford and no one then knew where or what that was,
      and thought him strange,
and Linda whose enduring pleasure was to walk her three khaki and cream collies in the sand,
  and ride her Palomino pony down Fairview Avenue on Saturday afternoons, with me trailing on my chesnut white-blazed mare;
  the Linda who tore out her hair strand by strand,
  because of some nervous ailment afflicting those born during World War last;
and Alberto who never attained full growth for lack of food and mother's milk,
  slight slender his being he who led me to know
  that my life's leaving has begun:
I wonder where they're living now, and if they too are remembering Elsewhere's other autumns,
  As I do
  In Los Cabos.

About the Author

Tamar Diana Wilson combined poetry, creative non-fiction, and academic chapters in her *Subsidizing Capitalism: Brickmakers on the U.S.-Mexico Border* (Albany: SUNY Press, 2005). Her creative non-fiction collection *Tales from Colonia Popular* (Austin: Plain View Press) was published in 2009 as was her non-fiction *Women's Migration Networks in Mexico and Beyond* (Albuquerque: University of New Mexico Press). She has published articles on immigration, the informal sector, and gender issues in *Anthropological Quarterly, Critique of Anthropology, Journal of Borderlands Studies, Human Organization, Latin American Perspectives, Review of Radical Political Economics, Violence Against Women, and Urban Anthropology*. Her fiction and poetry have appeared in *Struggle, Anthropology & Humanism, Saturday Night Journal, Thema, Blue Mesa Review* and in two collections of poetry, one edited by Terry Wolverton and one by Candace Catlin Hall. She has lived in Mexico since 1988.

Keyi Village, near Kunming, China, July 2009. Photograph by Ziao Chenjun

www.ingramcontent.com/pod-product-compliance
Lightning Source LLC
Chambersburg PA
CBHW052103070526
44584CB00017B/2306